S0-BLE-150

THE BEST FROM THE BOTTLE

by Mark Schneider,
Greg Sadofsky,
Jeffrey Allan Wilson
and Julio Deulofeu

quick fox

New York · London

Copyright © 1979 by Jeffrey A. Wilson, Mark
Schneider, Julio R. Deuloufeu, and Greg Sadofsky
All rights reserved.

International Standard Book Number: 0-8256-3157-2
Library of Congress Catalog Card Number: 79-648 73

No part of this book may be reproduced or transmitted
in any form or by any means, electronic or mechanical,
including photocopying, without permission in writing
from the publisher: Quick Fox, A Division of Music
Sales Corporation, 33 West 60th Street, New York 10023.

In Great Britain: Book Sales Ltd., 78 Newman Street,
London W1P 3LA.
In Canada: Gage Trade Publishing, P.O. Box 5000,
164 Commander Blvd., Agincourt, Ontario M1S 3C7.

PRINTED IN JAPAN

INTRODUCTION

Dear Reader:

Have you ever heard of a Flaming Green Lizard or a Blue Tail Fly? Now you can learn how to make these and many others from this collection of over 350 sensational recipes. Discover the secrets bartenders across the world have used to make fascinating, mouth-watering drinks. Just a twist of lime or an extra splash of tonic or bitters can make all the difference in producing exciting new taste experiences for your mixed drinks repertoire.

We have experimented with just about every possible combination of liquors and added ingredients, and would like to share our discoveries with you. We bring together the most exotic and flavorful mixed drink recipes ever collected. These exciting recipes are so simple and easy-to-follow, you can make and enjoy current and fashionable mixed drinks at home!

We have included an illustrated guide to the best of today's glassware, a complete alphabetical index for quick reference, and a simple glossary of bar terminology. Everything you need to know about how to get *The Best from the Bottle* is here.

Cheers,

Mark Schneider   Greg Sadofsky
Jeffrey Allan Wilson   Julio Deulofeu

THE BEST OF GLASSWARE

A-1
A-2   OLD-FASHIONED or ROCK GLASS
Over the years, the Old-Fashioned glass has become a versatile and all-purpose glass. It is used for "on the rocks" drinks such as Mists, two-liquor drinks, and, of course, Old-Fashioneds.

B   COCKTAIL or UP GLASS
Martinis, Manhattans, and Rob Roys are examples of drinks that, after being chilled and strained, are poured into the cocktail glass.

C   HIGHBALL GLASS
This straight, thin glass holds about eight ounces of mixed drinks such as Gin and Tonic, Scotch and Soda, Vodka and Water.

D   COLLINS or TALL GLASS
Taller than the highball glass, the Collins glass has the same straight, thin shape. Used for Bloody Marys, Screwdrivers, Fizzes, Collins, and fruit drinks, the Collins glass is versatile.

E   SOUR GLASS
Usually stemmed, this glass is used for Whiskey, Rum, or Brandy Sours, as well as coffee drinks.

F   LIQUEUR, CORDIAL or PONY GLASS
The Liqueur glass is fragile, short, and narrow. It is used for holding liqueurs and cordials. The glass is also called a *pousse-cafe* for holding layers of different liqueurs.

G   SHOT GLASS
The Shot glass is used for measuring ingredients and for "shooting" (drinking) liquors straight, such as Tequila or Whiskey. It usually measures one to one-and-a-half ounces.

H-1,
H-2   BRANDY SNIFTER
Brandy snifters range from small, two-ounce snifters to large, twenty-five ounce balloon-shaped ones. Their rounded bowl is designed to retain the liquor's fragrance and to allow the drinker to nose it. The snifter is perfect for after-dinner liqueurs, such as Grand Marnier, Drambuie, and Ouzo.

I   **WINE GLASS**
The all-purpose wine glass is tulip-shaped for trapping the wine's bouquet and enabling the drinker to eye the color, to swirl the wine, and to nose it. The glass is never more than half-filled. It is used for both red and white wines, as well as champagne.

J   **PORT or SHERRY GLASS**
This squat Port glass is ideal for drinking Port or Sherry. Many variations on this glass are also used.

K-1,   **BEER GLASS**
K-2   The Beer mug (K-1) and Pilsner glass (K-2) are the most common containers used exclusively for drinking beer. The Pilsner glass retains cold and fizz as long as possible. The Beer mug is usually made with a weighted bottom.

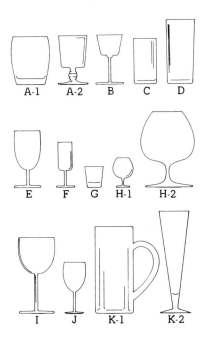

5

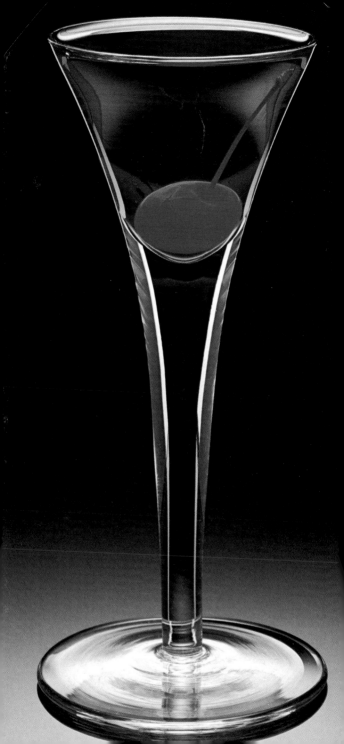

WHISKEY

1. AFFINITY COCKTAIL

1 oz. scotch
½ oz. dry vermouth
½ oz. sweet vermouth
2 dashes of bitters
Build in rock glass with cubed
ice. Garnish with red cherry
and lemon twist.

2. AGGRAVATION

1 oz. scotch
1 oz. Kahlúa
1 oz. heavy cream
Build in highball glass with
cubed ice.

3. BAMBINI-ARUBA

¾ oz. bourbon
¾ oz. vodka
¾ oz. rum
1½ oz. sweet-and-sour mix
¾ oz. orange juice
¾ oz. pineapple juice
½ oz. grenadine
Build in bucket glass with crushed
ice. Garnish with orange slice and
red cherry.

4. BARACUDA

¾ oz. bourbon
¼ oz. orgeat
¾ oz. orange juice
1½ oz. sweet-and-sour mix
Blend with crushed ice. Pour
into cocktail glass. Garnish
with red cherry.

WHISKEY

5. BARBARY COAST
½ oz. scotch
½ oz. gin
½ oz. white créme de cacao
½ oz. heavy cream
Blend with crushed ice. Pour
into cocktail glass.

6. BOILERMAKER
1 oz. bourbon
Cold beer
Serve bourbon in shot glass
with beer chaser on the side.

7. BOURBON-CASSIS COCKTAIL
1 oz. bourbon
½ oz. dry vermouth
¼ oz. créme de cassis
¼ oz. fresh lemon juice
Build in rock glass with cubed
ice. Garnish with lemon twist.

8. BOURBON MAI TAI
1¼ oz. bourbon
¾ oz. orange juice
¾ oz. pineapple juice
¾ oz. sweet-and-sour mix
¼ oz. grenadine
½ oz. orgeat
¼ oz. orange curaçao
Build in bucket glass with
crushed ice. Garnish with red
cherry and orange slice.

WHISKEY

9. BOURBON HIGHBALL
1¼ oz. bourbon
Water, ginger ale, soda, cola,
or 7-Up.
Build in highball glass. Fill with
chosen mixer.

10. BOURBON SOUR
1¼ oz. bourbon
2 dashes of bitters
Splash of soda
¼ teaspoon sugar
1 egg white
Blend with crushed ice. Pour into
cocktail glass. Garnish with red
cherry.

11. BRASS KNUCKLE
1 oz. bourbon
¼ oz. curaçao
1¼ oz. sweet-and-sour mix
Blend with crushed ice. Pour
into cocktail glass. Garnish with
red cherry.

12. BROWN FOX
1¼ oz. bourbon
½ oz. Benedictine
Build in rock glass with cubed
ice.

WHISKEY

13. CALIFORNIA LEMONAD

1¼ oz. bourbon
1½ oz. sweet-and-sour mix
¼ oz. grenadine
Blend with crushed ice. Pour
into sour glass. Garnish with
red cherry.

14. COWBOY

1¼ oz. bourbon
½ oz. heavy cream
Build in rock glass with cubed
ice.

15. DERBY FIZZ

1¼ oz. scotch
½ oz. sweet-and-sour mix
1 egg
¼ oz. curacao
Soda
Blend with crushed ice. Pour
into collins glass. Fill with soda.

16. DRY MANHATTAN

1¼ oz. bourbon
½ oz. dry vermouth
Build in rock glass with cubed
ice. Garnish with green olive.

17. DRY ROB ROY

1¼ oz. scotch
½ oz. dry vermouth
Build in rock glass with cubed
ice. Garnish with green olive.

WHISKEY

18. THE DUDE
1 oz. scotch
Dash of grenadine
¼ oz. Harvey's Bristol Cream
(float)
Build in rock glass with cubed
ice. Float Bristol Cream.

19. THE FANS
1 oz. scotch
¼ oz. cointreau
2 oz. grapefruit juice
Build in highball glass with
cubed ice.

20. FOX RIVER
1 oz. bourbon
¼ oz. white creme de cacao
2 dashes of bitters
Build in rock glass with cubed
ice.

21. FRENCH 95
1¼ oz. bourbon
1 oz. sweet-and-sour mix
½ oz. soda
Champagne
Build in collins glass with
crushed ice. Fill with champagne.

22. GODFATHER
¾ oz. scotch or bourbon
¾ oz. amaretto
Build in rock glass with cubed
ice.

WHISKEY

23. JOHN COLLINS

1¼ oz. bourbon
1½ oz. sweet-and-sour mix
7-Up
Build in collins glass with cubed
ice. Fill with 7-Up. Garnish with
red cherry.

24. LADY COCKTAIL

1 oz. bourbon
¼ oz. Pernod
¼ oz. anisette
Dash of bitters
Build in rock glass with cubed
ice.

25. MAMIE TAYLOR

1¼ oz. scotch
¼ oz. fresh lime juice
Ginger ale
Build in highball glass with
cubed ice. Fill with ginger ale.

26. MANHATTAN

1¼ oz. bourbon
½ oz. sweet vermouth
Build in rock glass with cubed
ice. Garnish with red cherry.

27. MASTER OF THE HOUNDS

1 oz. bourbon
¼ oz. cherry brandy
Dash of bitters
Build in rock glass with cubed ice.

28. MILLIONAIRE

1 oz. bourbon
½ oz. curaçao
1 egg white
Dash of grenadine
Blend with crushed ice. Pour
into cocktail glass.

29. MINT JULEP

1¼ oz. bourbon
¼ oz. green créme de menthe
Splash of water
Build in highball glass with
cubed ice.

30. MORNING FIZZ

1¼ oz. bourbon
1 egg white
¾ oz. sweet-and-sour mix
¼ oz. Pernod
Soda
Blend with crushed ice. Pour
into collins glass. Fill with soda.

31. OLD-FASHIONED

2 dashes of bitters
½ teaspoon sugar
Splash of soda
1¼ oz. bourbon
Put sugar, bitters, and soda in
rock glass. Build with cubed ice.
Garnish with red cherry, lemon
twist, and orange slice.

WHISKEY

32. OLD ROB
¾ oz. scotch
¾ oz. sweet vermouth
¼ teaspoon sugar
Dash of bitters
Build in rock glass with cubed
ice.

33. ORANGE FASHIONED
½ teaspoon sugar
2 dashes of bitters
Splash of soda
1 oz. bourbon
½ oz. orange juice
Put sugar, bitters, and soda in
rock glass. Build with cubed
ice. Garnish with red cherry,
orange slice, and lemon twist.

34. PERFECT MANHATTAN
1¼ oz. bourbon
¼ oz. sweet vermouth
¼ oz. dry vermouth
Build in rock glass with cubed
ice. Garnish with lemon twist.

35. PERFECT ROB ROY
1¼ oz. scotch
¼ oz. sweet vermouth
¼ oz. dry vermouth
Build in rock glass with cubed
ice. Garnish with lemon twist.

WHISKEY

36. PINEAPPLE SOUR
1¼ oz. bourbon
2 oz. pineapple juice
¼ oz. sweet-and-sour mix
Blend with crushed ice. Pour
into cocktail glass.

37. PRESBYTERIAN
1¼ oz. bourbon
Ginger ale
Soda
Build in highball glass with cubed
ice. Fill ½ with ginger ale, ½ with
soda. Garnish with lemon twist.

38. RATTLESNAKE
1¼ oz. bourbon
Dash of anisette
1¼ oz. sweet-and-sour mix
1 egg white
Blend with crushed ice. Pour
into cocktail glass.

39. ROB ROY
1¼ oz. scotch
½ oz. sweet vermouth
Build in rock glass with cubed
ice. Garnish with red cherry.

40. RUBY
1 oz. bourbon
½ oz. red Dubonnet
¼ oz. cointreau
Build in rock glass with cubed
ice. Garnish with lemon twist.

WHISKEY

41. RUSTY NAIL
¾ oz. scotch
¾ oz. Drambuie
Build in rock glass with cubed ice.

42. SAZERAC
½ teaspoon sugar
2 dashes of bitters
1¼ oz. bourbon
¼ oz. anisette (float)
Put sugar and bitters in rock glass. Build with cubed ice. Float anisette. Garnish with lemon twist.

43. SCOTCH COLLINS
1¼ oz. scotch
1½ oz. sweet-and-sour mix
7-Up
Build in collins glass with cubed ice. Garnish with red cherry.

44. SCOTCH-FASHIONED
½ teaspoon sugar
2 dashes of bitters
Splash of soda
1¼ oz. scotch
Put sugar, bitters, and soda in rock glass. Build with cubed ice. Garnish with red cherry, lemon twist, and orange slice.

45. SCOTCH HIGHBALL
1¼ oz. scotch
Water or soda
Build in highball glass with cubed
ice. Fill with water or soda.

46. SCOTCH MILK PUNCH
1¼ oz. scotch
4 oz. milk
1 teaspoon sugar
Build in collins glass with cubed
ice.

47. SCOTCH MINT COOLER
1¼ oz. scotch
¼ oz. white créme de menthe
Soda
Build in highball glass with cubed
ice. Fill with soda.

48. SCOTCH SIDECAR
1¼ oz. scotch
½ oz. cointreau
1½ oz. sweet-and-sour mix
Blend with crushed ice. Pour into
cocktail glass rimmed with sugar.

49. SCOTCH SOUR
1¼ oz. scotch
1¼ oz. sweet-and-sour mix
Blend with crushed ice. Pour
into sour glass. Garnish with red
cherry.

WHISKEY

50. SNOWSHOE
1 oz. Wild Turkey
¼ oz. 151-proof rum (float)
Serve in shot glass. Float rum.

51. SOUTHERN SOUR
¾ oz. bourbon
¾ oz. Southern Comfort
1½ oz. sweet-and-sour mix
Blend with crushed ice. Pour
into cocktail glass. Garnish with
red cherry.

52. STAIRCASE
1 oz. scotch
¼ oz. dry vermouth
¼ oz. sweet vermouth
¼ oz. Drambuie
Build in rock glass with cubed
ice.

53. T.N.T.
¾ oz. bourbon
¾ oz. anisette
Build in rock glass with cubed
ice.

54. TASTE OF HONEY
1 oz. scotch
½ oz. honey
1 oz. heavy cream
Blend with crushed ice. Pour
into cocktail glass.

WHISKEY

55. WHISKEY FLIP
1¼ oz. bourbon
1 egg
1 teaspoon sugar
Blend with crushed ice. Pour into
cocktail glass. Garnish with
sprinkle of nutmeg.

56. WHISKEY MILK PUNCH
1¼ oz. bourbon
3 oz. heavy cream
1 teaspoon sugar
Build in collins glass with cubed
ice.

57. WHISKEY SOUR
1¼ oz. bourbon
1½ oz. sweet-and-sour mix
Blend with crushed ice. Pour
into sour glass. Garnish with red
cherry.

58. YELLOW ROSE
1 oz. bourbon
½ oz. apple brandy
1½ oz. sweet-and-sour mix
Blend with crushed ice. Pour into
sour glass. Garnish with red
cherry.

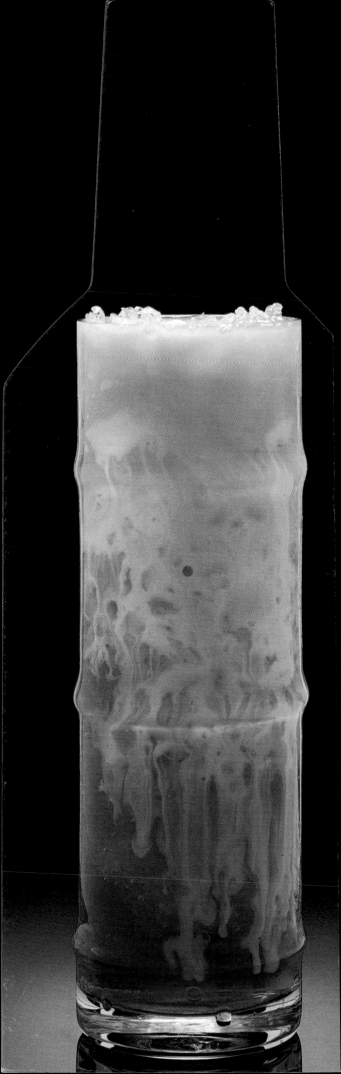

BRANDY

59. APPLE BLOSSOM

1½ oz. apple brandy
1½ oz. apple juice
1½ oz. sweet-and-sour mix
Blend with crushed ice. Pour
into sour glass.

60. APPLECAR

1 oz. apple brandy
½ oz. cointreau
1 oz. sweet-and-sour mix
Blend with crushed ice. Pour
into sour glass.

61. APPLE SUNRISE

1¼ oz. apple brandy
1½ oz. orange juice
1 oz. sweet-and-sour mix
¼ oz. grenadine
Build in collins glass with
crushed ice. Float grenadine.
Garnish with orange wedge and
red cherry.

62. BEN BRANDY

1¼ oz. brandy
½ oz. Benedictine
½ oz. orange juice
Build in rock glass with cubed
ice. Garnish with red cherry.

63. BRANANA

1 oz. brandy
1 oz. créme de bananes
1 oz. sweet-and-sour mix
Blend with crushed ice. Pour
into sour glass.

BRANDY

64. BETWEEN THE SHEETS
½ oz. brandy
½ oz. rum
½ oz. triple sec
1 oz. sweet-and-sour mix
Blend with crushed ice. Pour
into sour glass.

65. BRANDIED APRICOT
¾ oz. brandy
¾ oz. apricot brandy
1 oz. sweet-and-sour mix
Blend with crushed ice. Pour
into sour glass. Garnish with
orange wedge.

66. BRANDY ALEXANDER
¾ oz. brandy
¾ oz. dark créme de cacao
1 oz. heavy cream
Blend with crushed ice. Pour
into wine glass. Garnish with
sprinkle of nutmeg.

67. BRANDY OLD-FASHIONED
½ teaspoon sugar
2 dashes of bitters
Splash of soda
1¼ oz. brandy
Put sugar, bitters and soda in
rock glass. Fill with cubed ice.
Build with brandy. Garnish with
red cherry, lemon twist, and
orange slice.

BRANDY

68. BRANDY COLLINS
1¼ oz. brandy
2 oz. sweet-and-sour mix
7-Up
Build in collins glass with cubed ice. Fill with 7-Up. Garnish with orange wedge and red cherry.

69. BRANDY HIGHBALL
1¼ oz. brandy
Water or soda
Build in highball glass with cubed ice. Fill with water or soda.
Optional garnish: lemon twist.

70. BRANDY MANHATTAN
1½ oz. brandy
¼ oz. sweet vermouth
Build in rock glass. Or serve up in martini glass. Garnish with red cherry.

71. BRANDY MILK PUNCH
1¼ oz. brandy
1 teaspoon sugar
6 oz. heavy cream
Blend with crushed ice. Pour into collins glass. Garnish with sprinkle of nutmeg.

72. BRANDY MINT BUCK
1¼ oz. brandy
¼ oz. white créme de menthe
½ oz. fresh lemon juice
Ginger ale
Build in collins glass with cubed ice. Fill with ginger ale.

BRANDY

73. BRANDY CASSIS

1¼ oz. brandy
½ oz. fresh lemon juice
¼ oz. créme de cassis (float)
Build in rock glass. Garnish
with lemon twist.

74. BRANDY SOUR

1¼ oz. brandy
1½ oz. sweet-and-sour mix
½ oz. orange juice
Blend with crushed ice. Pour
into sour glass. Garnish with
red cherry.

75. BRANTINI

1½ oz. brandy
¾ teaspoon dry vermouth
Build in rock glass. Or serve up
in martini glass. Garnish with
lemon twist.

76. BROWN DERBY

¾ oz. brandy
¾ oz. Vandermint
¾ oz. heavy cream
Build in rock glass with cubed
ice.

77. CHERRY BLOSSOM

1 oz. brandy
¾ oz. cherry brandy
¼ oz. curaçao
¾ teaspoon grenadine
Build in highball glass with cubed
ice. Fill with soda; stir. Garnish
with red cherry.

BRANDY

78. DIRTY MOTHER
3¼ oz. brandy
¾ oz. Kahlúa
Build in rock glass with crushed
ice.

79. FRENCH 125
1¼ oz. brandy
1 oz. sweet-and-sour mix
½ oz. soda
Champagne
Build in collins glass with
crushed ice. Fill with champagne.

80. FRUIT-BRANDY SOUR
1¼ oz. fruit brandy (apple,
apricot, blackberry, cherry, or
peach)
2 oz. sweet-and-sour mix
Blend with crushed ice. Pour
into sour glass. Garnish with
red cherry.

81. GREEK STINGER
1¼ oz. Metaxa
½ oz. white créme de menthe
Build in rock glass with cubed
ice.

82. HOT TODDY
1½ oz. brandy
½ oz. fresh lemon juice
½ teaspoon sugar
Hot water
Pour into coffee mug. Fill mug
with hot water. Garnish with
sprinkle of nutmeg and
cinnamon.

BRANDY

83. INTERNATIONAL STINGER
1 oz. Metaxa
½ oz. Galliano
Build in rock glass with cubed ice.

84. JACK ROSE
1¼ oz. apple brandy
1½ oz. sweet-and-sour mix
¼ oz. grenadine
Blend with crushed ice. Pour into sour glass.

85. JELLY BEAN
¾ oz. cherry brandy
⅓ oz. anisette (float)
Serve in shot glass. Float anisette.

86. MEEK GREEK
1¼ oz. Metaxa
¼ oz. ouzo
½ oz. fresh lemon juice
Ginger ale
Build in collins glass with cubed ice. Fill with ginger ale.

BRANDY

87. MOON DROP

1¼ oz. apple brandy
½ oz. banana liqueur
1½ oz. sweet-and-sour mix
Blend with crushed ice. Pour
into sour glass.

88. ORANGE BRANDY COOLER

1 oz. brandy
½ oz. cherry brandy
½ oz. curaçao
2 oz. orange juice
Soda
Build in collins glass with cubed
ice. Fill with soda. Garnish with
orange wedge.

89. ORANGE CUP

½ oz. brandy
1 oz. orange juice
1 oz. cream sherry
½ oz. cointreau
1 oz. heavy cream
Blend with crushed ice. Pour
into wine glass.

90. SEPARATOR OR DIRTY WHITE MOTHER

1 oz. brandy
1 oz. Kahlúa
1 oz. heavy cream
Build in highball glass with
crushed ice.

BRANDY

91. SIDECAR

1¼ oz. brandy
½ oz. triple sec
1½ oz. sweet-and-sour mix
Blend with crushed ice. Pour
into cocktail glass rimmed with
sugar.

92. SIR WARSHAW COCKTAIL

¾ oz. dark rum
¾ oz. brandy
¾ teaspoon grenadine
¾ teaspoon curaçao
¼ oz. sweet-and-sour mix
Blend with crushed ice. Pour
into bucket glass. Garnish with
red cherry.

93. SLOE BRANDY

1¼ oz. brandy
½ oz. sloe gin
¾ teaspoon fresh lemon juice
Serve up in cocktail glass.

94. STINGER

1¼ oz. brandy
½ oz. white créme de menthe
(float)
Build in rock glass with cubed
ice. Float créme de menthe.

BRANDY

95. THUMPER

1½ oz. brandy
¾ oz. Tuaca
Build in rock glass. Garnish with
lemon twist.

96. APPLE SAUCE
1 oz. gin
¾ oz. apple brandy
¾ teaspoon grenadine
1 oz. sweet-and-sour mix
1 oz. orange juice
Blend with crushed ice. Pour into sour glass. Garnish with red cherry.

97. BERMUDA COCKTAIL
1 oz. gin
¾ oz. peach brandy
¼ oz. grenadine
¼ oz. orange juice
Blend with crushed ice. Pour into cocktail glass.

98. BERMUDA ROSE COCKTAIL
1 oz. gin
¾ oz. apricot brandy
¼ oz. grenadine
Blend with crushed ice. Pour into cocktail glass.

99. BLACK ROSE
¾ oz. gin
¾ oz. blackberry brandy
¾ oz. sweet-and-sour mix
Blend with crushed ice. Pour into sour glass.

100. BLUE DEVIL
1¼ oz. gin
½ oz. blue curacao
½ oz. sweet-and-sour mix
Blend with crushed ice. Pour
into cocktail glass. Garnish with
lemon twist.

101. CHINAMAN'S HAT
1 oz. gin
½ oz. Cherry Heering
1 oz. sweet-and-sour mix
Créme de cassis (float)
Build in highball glass with
cubed ice. Float créme de cassis.

102. CAMPARI COCKTAIL
¾ oz. gin
¾ oz. green crème de menthe
¾ oz. Campari
Build in rock glass with
cubed ice.

103. CUCUMBER
¾ oz. gin
¾ oz. green créme de menthe
¾ oz. heavy cream
Build in rock glass with cubed
ice.

104. DEPTH CHARGE
1 oz. gin
½ oz. triple sec
2 dashes of anisette (float)
Blend with crushed ice. Pour
into wine glass. Float anisette.

105. DUBONNET COCKTAIL
1¼ oz. gin
½ oz. red Dubonnet
Chill in mixing glass with cubed
ice. Stir and drain into martini
glass. Or build in rock glass with
cubed ice. Garnish with lemon
twist.

106. FOGGY DAY
1¼ oz. gin
½ oz. Pernod
Build in rock glass with cubed
ice. Garnish with lemon twist.

107. FRENCH 75
1¼ oz. gin
1 oz. sweet-and-sour mix
½ oz. soda
Champagne
Build in collins glass with
crushed ice. Fill with champagne.

108. GIN BUCK
1¼ oz. gin
Ginger ale
Build in highball glass with
cubed ice. Fill with ginger ale.
Garnish with squeeze of lime.

109. GIMLET
1¼ oz. gin
½ oz. Rose's Lime Juice
Blend with crushed ice. Serve
in wine glass. Garnish with
green cherry.

GIN

110. GIBSON
1½ oz. gin
½ oz. dry vermouth
Chill in mixing glass with cubed ice. Stir and drain into martini glass. Or build in rock glass with cubed ice. Garnish with cocktail onion.

111. GIN FIZZ
1¼ oz. gin
1 oz. sweet-and-sour mix
¼ oz. fresh lime juice
Soda
Blend with crushed ice. Strain and pour into sour glass. Fill with soda.

112. GIN PUNCH
1 oz. gin
1 oz. coconut milk
½ oz. Cherry Heering
1 oz. orange juice
1 oz. pineapple juice
Blend with crushed ice. Pour into collins glass. Garnish with orange slice and red cherry.

113. GIN-LICORICE COCKTAIL
¾ oz. gin
¾ oz. anisette
1 teaspoon sugar
1 egg white
Blend with crushed ice. Pour into cocktail glass.

114. GIN HIGHBALL
1¼ oz. gin
Tonic, 7-Up or soda
Build in highball glass with
cubed ice. Fill with choice of
mixer. Garnish with lime wedge.

115. GIN RICKY
1¼ oz. gin
Soda
Build in highball glass with cubed
ice. Fill with soda. Garnish with
squeeze of lime.

116. GIN ROSE
1¼ oz. gin
1¼ oz. sweet-and-sour mix
¼ oz. grenadine
Blend with crushed ice. Pour
into sour glass. Garnish with
red cherry.

117. GIN-SCOTCH MARTINI
1½ oz. gin
½ oz. scotch
Chill in mixing glass with cubed
ice. Stir and strain into martini
glass. Or build in rock glass with
cubed ice. Garnish with lemon
twist.

118. GIN SOUR
1¼ oz. gin
1½ oz. sweet-and-sour mix
Blend with crushed ice. Strain
and pour into sour glass. Garnish
with red cherry.

119. GIN-SHERRY MARTINI

1¼ oz. gin
½ oz. dry sherry
Chill in mixing glass with cubed
ice. Stir and drain into martini
glass. Or build in rock glass with
cubed ice. Garnish with lemon
twist.

120. GOLDEN FIZZ

1½ oz. gin
¾ oz. sweet-and-sour mix
2 oz. heavy cream
1 egg yolk
1 teaspoon sugar
Soda
Blend with crushed ice. Pour
into collins glass. Fill with soda.

121. GRAND SLAM

1 oz. gin
¼ oz. Grand Marnier
1 oz. orange juice
¾ teaspoon grenadine
Blend with crushed ice. Pour
into sour glass. Garnish with
red cherry.

122. GREENTINI

1¼ oz. gin
½ oz. green créme de menthe
Build in rock glass with cubed
ice.

GIN

123. GREAT DANE

1¼ oz. gin
½ oz. triple sec
1 oz. orange juice
1 oz. sweet-and-sour mix
Blend with crushed ice. Pour
into sour glass. Garnish with
red cherry.

124. HARLEM COCKTAIL

1¼ oz. gin
1½ oz. pineapple juice
¼ oz. Cherry Heering
Blend with crushed ice. Pour
into sour glass. Garnish with
red cherry.

125. HONOLULU COCKTAIL

1¼ oz. gin
1 oz. orange juice
1 oz. pineapple juice
½ oz. sweet-and-sour mix
Blend with crushed ice. Pour
into bucket glass. Garnish with
red cherry.

126. HULA-HULA

1¼ oz. gin
1¼ oz. orange juice
¼ oz. curaçao
Build in rock glass with cubed
ice.

127. MARTINI

The martini is one of the most popular cocktails. Today the preference is for drier martinis; that is, less vermouth. A martini must be served ice cold. This is best accomplished by stirring it in a mixing glass. The dilution makes for a smoother and more palatable drink. Here are some variations:

1. 3 to 1
1½ oz. gin
½ oz. dry vermouth
Chill in mixing glass with cubed ice. Stir and drain into martini glass. Garnish with green olive. Lemon twist optional.

2. 4 to 1
1½ oz. gin
⅜ oz. dry vermouth

3. 6 to 1
1½ oz. gin
¼ oz. dry vermouth

4. 8 to 1
2 oz. gin
¼ oz. dry vermouth

Note: Any of the above can be built in rock glass with cubed ice.

128. NEGRONE

¾ oz. gin
½ oz. Campari
½ oz. sweet vermouth
Chill in mixing glass with cubed ice. Strain and pour into cocktail glass. Garnish with lemon twist.

129. ORANGE BLOSSOM

1 oz. gin
1½ oz. orange juice
1 teaspoon sugar
Blend with crushed ice. Pour
into cocktail glass.

130. ORANGE GIMLET

1¼ oz. gin
¼ oz. Rose's Lime Juice
½ oz. orange juice
¼ oz. fresh lime juice
Blend with crushed ice. Pour
into wine glass. Garnish with
orange slice and green cherry.

131. ORGEAT COCKTAIL

1¼ oz. gin
1¼ oz. orange juice
¼ oz. orgeat (almond-flavored
syrup)
Blend with crushed ice. Pour
into cocktail glass.

132. PINEAPPLE MINT COOLER

¾ oz. gin
¾ oz. green créme de menthe
2 oz. pineapple juice
Build in collins glass with
crushed ice.

133. PINK SKY

1¼ oz. gin
1½ oz. sweet-and-sour mix
¼ oz. grenadine
Blend with crushed ice. Pour
into sour glass.

134. RAMOS FIZZ

1½ oz. gin
¾ oz. sweet-and-sour mix
2 oz. heavy cream
1 teaspoon sugar
1 egg white
¼ oz. orange juice
Soda
Blend with crushed ice. Pour
into collins glass. Fill with soda.

135. RED DERBY

1 oz. gin
½ oz. apricot brandy
½ oz. fresh lemon juice
¾ teaspoon grenadine
Blend with crushed ice. Pour
into sour glass. Garnish with
red cherry.

136. ROYAL FIZZ

1½ oz. gin
¾ oz. sweet-and-sour mix
2 oz. heavy cream
1 egg
1 teaspoon sugar
Soda
Blend with crushed ice. Pour
into collins glass. Fill with soda.

137. SILVER FIZZ

1½ oz. gin
¾ oz. sweet-and-sour mix
2 oz. heavy cream
1 egg white
1 teaspoon sugar
Soda
Blend with crushed ice. Pour
into collins glass. Fill with soda.

138. SINGAPORE SLING
1¼ oz. gin
1¾ oz. sweet-and-sour mix
½ oz. soda
¼ oz. cherry brandy (float)
¼ oz. grenadine (float)
Build in collins glass with crushed ice. Add soda. Float brandy and grenadine. Garnish with red cherry.

139. SLOEBERRY SLING
1¼ oz. sloe gin
1¾ oz. sweet-and-sour mix
Soda
¼ oz. cherry brandy (float)
Build in collins glass with crushed ice. Fill with soda. Float brandy. Garnish with red cherry.

140. SLOE GIN FIZZ
1¼ oz. sloe gin
1½ oz. sweet-and-sour mix
Soda
Blend with crushed ice. Strain and pour into sour glass. Fill with soda.

141. SPARROW
¾ oz. gin
¾ oz. apricot brandy
1½ oz. heavy cream
Build in highball glass with cubed ice.

142. TOM COLLINS
1¼ oz. gin
1½ oz. sweet-and-sour mix
7-Up
Build in collins glass with cubed ice. Fill with 7-Up. Garnish with red cherry.

41

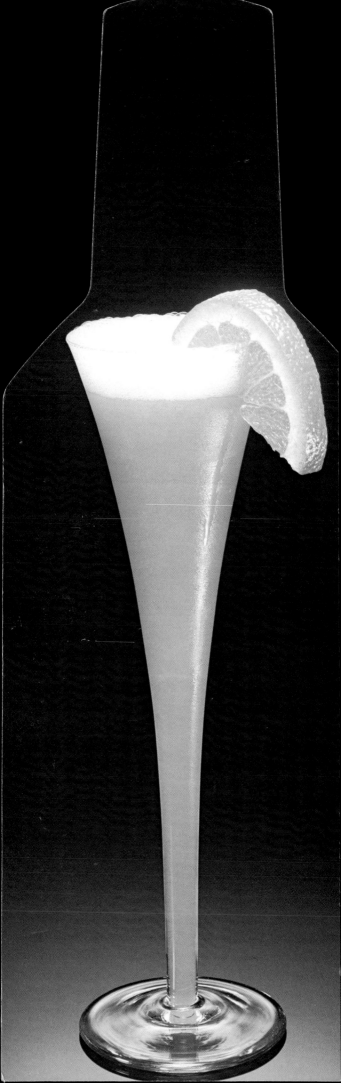

143. APPLE CORE

1¼ oz. rum
1¼ oz. apple juice
1 oz. sweet-and-sour mix
Blend with crushed ice. Pour
into cocktail glass. Garnish
with red cherry.

144. BACARDI COCKTAIL

1¼ oz. Bacardi rum
1½ oz. sweet-and-sour mix
¼ oz. grenadine
Blend with crushed ice. Pour
into sour glass. Garnish with
red cherry.

145. BANANA DAIQUIRI

1¼ oz. rum
1¼ oz. sweet-and-sour mix
¼ oz. banana liqueur
1 banana
Blend with crushed ice. Pour
into sour glass.

146. BANANA SPLIT

1¼ oz. rum
1 banana
½ oz. créme de bananes
1 oz. heavy cream
Blend with crushed ice. Pour
into bucket glass.

147. BETWEEN THE SHEETS

¾ oz. rum
¾ oz. brandy
½ oz. triple sec
1½ oz. sweet-and-sour mix
Blend with crushed ice. Pour
into cocktail glass.

43

RUM

148. BOLO
1¼ oz. rum
1 oz. sweet-and-sour mix
1 oz. orange juice
Blend with crushed ice. Pour
into cocktail glass. Garnish with
red cherry.

149. BOLO-BANGER
1¼ oz. rum
1 oz. orange juice
1 oz. sweet-and-sour mix
¼ oz. Galliano (float)
Build in collins glass with
crushed ice. Float Galliano.
Garnish with red cherry.

150. CALCULATOR
¾ oz. rum
¾ oz. Tia Maria
¾ oz. heavy cream
Build in rock glass with cubed
ice.

151. CASTRO COOLER
¾ oz. rum
¾ oz. apple brandy
1 oz. orange juice
¾ oz. sweet-and-sour mix
¼ oz. grenadine
Blend with crushed ice. Pour
into bucket glass. Garnish with
red cherry and orange slice.

RUM

152. COCO BOWL
1¼ oz. rum
1½ oz. coconut milk
1½ oz. pineapple juice
Blend with crushed ice. Pour
into wine glass.

153. COCONUT COOLER
1¼ oz. rum
2 oz. coconut milk
½ oz. heavy cream
Blend with crushed ice. Pour
into wine glass.

154. COCONUT DAIQUIRI
1¼ oz. rum
1¼ oz. sweet-and-sour mix
2 oz. coconut milk
Blend with crushed ice. Pour
into sour glass.

155. CORAL SEA
1¼ oz. rum
½ oz. curaçao
1 egg white
2 oz. pineapple juice
¼ oz. grenadine
Blend with crushed ice. Pour
into sour glass. Garnish with
red cherry.

156. CUBA LIBRE
1¼ oz. rum
Cola
Build in highball glass with cubed
ice. Fill with cola. Garnish with
squeeze of lime.

157. DAIQUIRI

1¼ oz. rum
1½ oz. sweet-and-sour mix
Blend with crushed ice. Pour
into sour glass. Garnish with
red cherry.

158. GOLDEN COLADA

1 oz. rum
½ oz. Galliano
1 oz. coconut milk
¾ oz. pineapple juice
¾ oz. orange juice
¼ oz. curaçao
Blend with crushed ice. Pour
into bucket glass. Garnish with
red cherry and orange slice.

159. HAVANA COCKTAIL

1¼ oz. rum
½ oz. sweet-and-sour mix
2 oz. pineapple juice
Blend with crushed ice. Pour
into sour glass. Garnish with
red cherry.

160. HOGBACK GROWLER

¾ oz. 151-proof rum
¼ oz. Metaxa
Serve in shot glass. Recommended
dosage: two per evening.

161. HOUND DOG

1¼ oz. rum
Grapefruit juice
Build in collins glass with cubed
ice. Fill with grapefruit juice.

RUM

162. ISLANDER
1¼ oz. rum
1 oz. papaya juice
1 oz. pineapple juice
1 oz. coconut juice
Blend with crushed ice. Pour
into bucket glass. Garnish with
red cherry.

163. JAMAICAN DRIVER
1¼ oz. rum
Orange juice
Build in collins glass with cubed
ice. Fill with orange juice.

164. JAMAICAN HAZE
1 oz. rum
½ oz. apricot brandy
1½ oz. sweet-and-sour mix
Blend with crushed ice. Pour
into sour glass. Garnish with
red cherry.

165. JAMAICAN SHAKE
1¼ oz. rum
1 scoop vanilla ice cream
1 oz. pineapple juice
¼ oz. grenadine
1 oz. heavy cream
Blend with crushed ice. Pour
into bucket glass.

166. JAMAICAN YO-YO
¾ oz. rum
¾ oz. Tia Maria
Build in rock glass with
cubed ice.

167. A LULU

1 oz. rum
½ oz. Galliano
¾ teaspoon créme de noyau
2 oz. orange juice
2 oz. pineapple juice
Blend with crushed ice. Pour
into bucket glass. Garnish with
red cherry and orange slice.

168. MAI TAI

1 oz. light rum
1 oz. Myers's Rum
¾ oz. orange juice
¾ oz. pineapple juice
¾ oz. sweet-and-sour mix
¼ oz. grenadine
½ oz. orgeat
¼ oz. orange curacao
Build in bucket glass with
crushed ice. Garnish with red
cherry and orange slice.

169. MELON-COLY

1¼ oz. rum
½ cup diced, seeded watermelon
½ oz. pineapple juice
2 dashes of grenadine
Blend with crushed ice. Pour
into collins glass. Fill with cubed ice.

170. MOON PIE

1¼ oz. rum
½ canned peach
1 oz. peach syrup
½ oz. créme de bananes
½ banana
1 oz. orange juice
Blend with crushed ice. Pour
into collins glass. Garnish with
red cherry and orange slice.

171. PEACH PIE

1¼ oz. rum
½ canned peach
1 oz. peach syrup
¾ oz. pineapple juice
Blend with crushed ice. Pour
into collins glass.

172. PIÑA COLADA

1¼ oz. rum
¾ oz. orange juice
1 oz. coconut milk
¾ oz. pineapple juice
¼ oz. curaçao
Blend with crushed ice. Pour
into bucket glass. Garnish with
red cherry and orange slice.

173. PINEAPPLE DAIQUIRI

1¼ oz. rum
1¼ oz. sweet-and-sour mix
2 oz. pineapple juice
Blend with crushed ice. Pour
into sour glass.

174. PLANTER'S PUNCH

1¼ Myers's Rum
¾ oz. orange juice
¾ oz. pineapple juice
¼ oz. Rose's Lime Juice
¼ oz. grenadine
Build in bucket glass with
crushed ice. Garnish with red
cherry and orange slice.

175. RAINBOW

1 oz. rum
¾ oz. créme de bananes
1 oz. coconut milk
1 oz. orange juice
Blend with crushed ice. Pour
into bucket glass. Garnish with
red cherry and orange slice.

176. RUMARITA

1¼ oz. rum
½ oz. cointreau
1½ oz. sweet-and-sour mix
Blend with crushed ice. Pour
into cocktail glass.

177. RUM COLLINS

1¼ oz. rum
1½ oz. sweet-and-sour mix
7-Up
Build in collins glass with cubed
ice. Fill with 7-Up. Garnish
with red cherry.

178. RUM GIMLET

1¼ oz. rum
½ oz. Rose's Lime Juice
Splash of soda
Blend with crushed ice. Pour
into wine glass. Add soda.
Garnish with green cherry.

179. RUM HIGHBALL

1¼ oz. rum
Cola, tonic, soda, water, or 7-Up
Build in highball glass with cubed
ice. Fill with chosen mixer.

180. RUM NOG
1¼ oz. rum
1 egg
4 oz. milk
1 teaspoon sugar
Dash of vanilla
Blend with crushed ice. Pour
into wine glass. Garnish with
sprinkle of nutmeg.

181. RUM-RISE
1¼ oz. rum
1½ oz. orange juice
½ oz. sweet-and-sour mix
Dash of grenadine (float)
¼ oz. créme de cassis (float)
Build in collins glass with
crushed ice. Or blend with
crushed ice and pour into
collins glass. Float grenadine
and créme de cassis. Garnish
with red cherry.

182. RUM SEPARATOR
1 oz. rum
1 oz. Kahlúa
1 oz. heavy cream
Build in highball glass with
cubed ice.

183. SCORPION
1¼ oz. rum
¾ oz. brandy
½ oz. orgeat
2 oz. orange juice
1½ oz. sweet-and-sour mix
Build in bucket glass with
crushed ice. Garnish with red
cherry and orange slice.

184. SOUTH SEAS

1 oz. rum
¼ oz. white créme de menthe
2 oz. pineapple juice
Blend with crushed ice. Pour
into wine glass. Garnish with
green cherry.

185. STRAWBERRY DAIQUIR

1¼ oz. rum
1¼ oz. sweet-and-sour mix
2 oz. thawed frozen strawberries
(fruit and syrup)
Blend with crushed ice. Pour
into sour glass.

186. TANGERINE

1¼ oz. rum
¼ oz. curaçao
2 oz. pineapple juice
¼ oz. grenadine
1 egg white
Blend with crushed ice. Pour
into bucket glass. Garnish with
red cherry and orange slice.

187. TROPICAL SHAKE

1¼ oz. rum
1 oz. pineapple juice
½ oz. green créme de menthe
1 oz. heavy cream
1 scoop vanilla ice cream
Blend with crushed ice. Pour
into bucket glass.

188. ZOMBIE

¾ oz. light rum
¾ oz. Myers's Rum
¾ oz. Don Q Gold Rum
¾ oz. sweet-and-sour mix
¾ oz. orange juice
¾ oz. pineapple juice
½ oz. grenadine
¼ oz. 151-proof rum (float)

Build in bucket glass with crushed ice. Float rum. Garnish with red cherry and orange slice.

TEQUILA

189. BANANA PANTHER
1¼ oz. tequila
2 sweet-and-sour mix
1 banana
Blend with crushed ice. Pour
into sour glass.

190. BLACKBERRY TEQUILA SOUR
1 oz. tequila
¾ oz. blackberry brandy
1½ oz. sweet-and-sour mix
Blend with crushed ice. Pour
into sour glass. Garnish with
red cherry.

191. BLACK BULL
¾ oz. tequila
¾ oz. Vandermint
Build in rock glass.

192. BRAVE BULL
¾ oz. tequila
¾ oz. Kahlúa
Build in rock glass.

193. COCONUT MARGARITA
1¼ oz. tequila
½ oz. triple sec
1 oz. sweet-and-sour mix
2 oz. coconut milk
Blend with crushed ice. Serve
in cocktail glass.

TEQUILA

194. DECEIVER
1 oz. tequila
½ oz. Galliano
Build in rock glass with cubed ice.

195. FREDDY FUDD
1¼ oz. tequila
2½ oz. orange juice
½ oz. Galliano
Build in collins glass with cubed ice.

196. GREEN BEAN
¾ oz. tequila
¾ oz. green créme de menthe
Build in rock glass with cubed ice.

197. ITALIAN SUNBURST
1¼ oz. tequila
¼ oz. triple sec
¾ teaspoon fresh lime juice
¼ oz. Galliano
2 oz. orange juice
Blend with crushed ice. Pour into bucket glass.

198. LATIN CONNECTION
1¼ oz. tequila
¼ oz. triple sec
1 oz. fresh lime juice
2 oz. pineapple juice
Blend with crushed ice. Pour into bucket glass.

TEQUILA

199. MARGARITA
1¼ oz. tequila
½ oz. triple sec
¼ to ½ oz. Rose's Lime Juice
1½ oz. sweet-and-sour mix
Blend with crushed ice. Serve in
cocktail glass rimmed with salt.

200. MEXICAN ALMOND
¾ oz. tequila
¾ oz. amaretto
Build in rock glass with cubed
ice.

201. MEXICAN BANANA
¾ oz. tequila
¾ oz. créme de bananes
¼ oz. white créme de cacao
¾ oz. heavy cream
Blend with crushed ice. Pour
into wine glass.

202. MEXICAN GREYHOUND
1¼ oz. tequila
Grapefruit juice
Build in highball glass. Fill with
grapefruit juice.

203. MEXICAN MELON
1¼ oz. tequila
½ cup diced, seeded watermelon
1 oz. sweet-and-sour mix
¼ oz. créme de cassis
Blend with crushed ice. Pour
into sour glass. Garnish with
lemon twist.

TEQUILA

204. MEXICAN RED
¾ oz. tequila
¾ oz. Dubonnet
Build in rock glass with cubed
ice. Garnish with lemon twist.

205. PANTHER
1 oz. tequila
½ oz. sweet-and-sour mix
Build in rock glass with cubed
ice.

206. REVERSE MARGARITA
¾ oz. tequila
¼ oz. triple sec
¾ teaspoon Rose's Lime Juice
1 oz. sweet-and-sour mix
Dash of salt
Squeeze of lime
For the bold and daring. Place
drinker with his back toward
you and head tilted up; bib
recommended. Pour ingredients
into mouth of drinker. Have
drinker hold ingredients in
mouth, shake, and swallow.

207. SHOOTER, SHOT, OR TEQUILA HOOKER
1 oz. tequila
Salt
Lime or lemon wedge
Serve in shot glass. Place salt on
hand, lick salt, swallow tequila,
then suck lime or lemon. Best
way to savor fine tequila.

TEQUILA

208. SEPARATOR

1 oz. tequila
1 oz. Kahlúa
1 oz. heavy cream
Build in highball glass with cubed ice.

209. STRAWBERRY MARGARITA

1¼ oz. tequila
½ oz. triple sec
1½ sweet-and-sour mix
2 oz. thawed frozen strawberries (fruit and syrup)
Blend with crushed ice. Salted rim of glass is optional. Serve in cocktail glass.

210. TEQUICHI

1¼ oz. tequila
1½ oz. coconut milk
¾ oz. pineapple juice
Blend with crushed ice. Pour into sour glass.

211. TEQUILA BLOODY MARY

1¼ oz. tequila
1½ oz. tomato juice
1½ oz. beef bouillon
¾ teaspoon fresh lime juice
2 dashes of Worcestershire sauce
Dash of tabasco sauce
Black pepper
Celery salt
Salt
Build in collins glass with cubed ice. Garnish with lime wedge.

TEQUILA

212. TEQUILA BANGER

1¼ oz. tequila
2½ oz. orange juice
¼ oz. Galliano (float)
Build in collins glass with
crushed ice. Float Galliano.

213. TEQUILA COLADA

1¼ oz. tequila
¾ oz. orange juice
¾ oz. pineapple juice
½ oz. coconut milk
¼ oz. orange curaçao
Blend with crushed ice. Pour
into bucket glass. Garnish with
red cherry and orange slice.

214. TEQUILA COLLINS

1½ oz. tequila
1 oz. sweet-and-sour mix
7-Up
Build in collins glass with cubed
ice. Fill with 7-Up. Garnish with
red cherry.

215. TEQUILA DRIVER

1¼ oz. tequila
Orange juice
Build in collins glass with cubed
ice. Fill with orange juice.

216. TEQUILA GIMLET

1¼ oz. tequila
½ oz. Rose's Lime Juice
Blend with crushed ice. Serve in
wine glass. Garnish with green
cherry.

TEQUILA

217. TEQUILA HIGHBALL

1¼ oz. tequila
Tonic, 7-Up, or soda
Build in highball glass with cubed
ice. Fill with chosen mixer.
Garnish with lime slice.

218. TEQUILA MARY

1¼ oz. tequila .
3 oz. tomato juice
  ¾ teaspoon fresh lime juice
2 dashes of Worcestershire sauce
Dash of tabasco sauce
Black pepper
Celery salt
Salt
Build in collins glass with cubed
ice. Garnish with squeeze of lime.

219. TEQUILA OLD-FASHIONED

½ teaspoon sugar
2 dashes of bitters
Dash of soda
1¼ oz. tequila
Put sugar, bitters, and soda in
rock glass. Fill with cubed ice.
Build with tequila. Garnish with
red cherry, lemon twist, and
orange slice.

220. TEQUILA PUNCH

1¼ oz. tequila
1½ oz. pineapple juice
1½ oz. orange juice
  ½ oz. sweet-and-sour mix
Grenadine (float)
Blend with crushed ice. Pour
into sour glass. Float grenadine.

TEQUILA

221. TEQUILA ROSE

1¼ oz. tequila
1¼ oz. sweet-and-sour mix
¼ oz. grenadine
Blend with crushed ice. Pour
into sour glass.

222. TEQUILA SALTY DOG

1¼ oz. tequila
2½ oz. grapefruit juice
Build in salt-rimmed collins
glass with cubed ice. Fill with
grapefruit juice.

223. TEQUILA SLING

1 oz. tequila
2 oz. sweet-and-sour mix
½ oz. soda
¼ oz. cherry brandy
¼ oz. sloe gin
Build in collins glass with
crushed ice. Garnish with red
cherry and orange slice.

224. TEQUILA SOUR

1¼ oz. tequila
1½ oz. sweet-and-sour mix
Blend with crushed ice. Pour
into sour glass. Garnish with
red cherry.

225. TEQUILA STINGER

1 oz. tequila
½ oz. white créme de menthe
Build in rock glass with cubed
ice.

TEQUILA

226. TEQUILA SUNRISE

1¼ oz. tequila
1½ oz. orange juice
½ oz. sweet-and-sour mix
Dash of grenadine (float)
¼ oz. créme de cassis (float)
Build in collins glass with
crushed ice. Or blend with
crushed ice and pour into
collins glass. Float grenadine
and créme de cassis. Garnish
with red cherry.

227. TEQUILA SUNSET

1¼ oz. tequila
¾ oz. orange juice
¾ oz. pineapple juice
¾ oz. coconut milk
¼ oz. sloe gin (float)
Build in collins glass with
crushed ice. Float sloe gin.

228. TEQUINI

1¼ oz. tequila
½ oz. dry vermouth
Build in rock glass with cubed
ice. Or serve up in martini glass.
Garnish with olive or lemon twist.

VODKA

229. BLACK CLOUD
¾ oz. vodka
¾ oz. Tia Maria
Build in rock glass with cubed
ice.

230. BLACK RUSSIAN
¾ oz. vodka
¾ oz. Kahlúa
Build in rock glass with cubed
ice.

231. BLENDED BANGER
1¼ oz. vodka
2 oz. orange juice
1 oz. heavy cream
½ oz. Galliano
Blend with crushed ice. Pour
into sour glass.

232. BLOODY BULL
1¼ oz. vodka
1½ oz. tomato juice
1½ oz. beef bouillon
¾ teaspoon fresh lime juice
2 dashes of Worcestershire sauce
Dash of tabasco sauce
Black pepper
Celery salt
Salt
Build in collins glass with cubed
ice. Garnish with squeeze of lime.

VODKA

233. BLOODY MARY

1¼ oz. vodka
3 oz. tomato juice
2 dashes of Worcestershire sauce
Dash of tabasco sauce
Black pepper
Celery salt
Salt
¾ teaspoon fresh lime juice
Build in collins glass with cubed
ice. Squeeze in lime juice.

234. BULLSHOT

1¼ oz. vodka
3 oz. beef bouillon
¾ teaspoon fresh lime juice
2 dashes of Worcestershire sauce
Dash of tabasco sauce
Black pepper
Celery salt
Salt
Build in collins glass with cubed
ice. Garnish with squeeze of lime.

235. CHOCOLATE RUSSIAN

¾ oz. vodka
¾ oz. Vandermint
Build in rock glass with cubed ice.

236. CHI-CHI

1¼ oz. vodka
2 oz. pineapple juice
2 oz. coconut milk
¼ oz. orange curaçao
Blend with crushed ice. Pour
into collins glass.

237. THE CZAR

¾ oz. vodka
¾ oz. Tuaca
Build in rock glass with cubed ice.

238. CHERRY DRIVER
¾ oz. vodka
¾ oz. cherry brandy
2 oz. orange juice
Build in collins glass with cubed ice. Garnish with red cherry and orange slice.

239. DANISH MARY
1¼ oz. aquavit
¾ teaspoon fresh lime juice
2 dashes of Worcestershire sauce
Dash of tabasco sauce
Black Pepper
Celery salt
Salt
Build in collins glass with cubed ice. Garnish with squeeze of lime.

240. FLYING GRASSHOPPER
¾ oz. vodka
¾ oz. green créme de menthe
¾ oz. white créme de cacao
Build in rock glass with cubed ice.

241. GODMOTHER
¾ oz. vodka
¾ oz. amaretto
Build in rock glass with cubed ice.

242. GREEN SPIDER
1¼ oz. vodka
½ oz. green créme de menthe
Build in rock glass with cubed ice.

VODKA

243. GREYHOUND
1¼ oz. vodka
Grapefruit juice
Build in collins glass with cubed
ice. Fill with grapefruit juice.

244. HARVEY WALLBANGER
1¼ oz. vodka
2½ oz. orange juice
¼ oz. Galliano (float)
Build in collins glass with
crushed ice. Float Galliano.

245. HI-RISE
1 oz. vodka
¼ oz. cointreau
2 oz. orange juice
1 oz. sweet-and-sour mix
¼ oz. grenadine
Blend with crushed ice. Pour
into bucket glass.

246. HURRICANE
1 oz. vodka
½ oz. anisette
Build in rock glass with cubed
ice.

247. ICE PICK
1¼ oz. vodka
1 teaspoon sugar
½ oz. fresh lemon juice
Iced tea
Build in collins glass with cubed
ice. Fill with iced tea.

248. JULIUS-DRIVER

¼ oz. vodka
3½ oz. orange juice
1 egg
2 teaspoons sugar
¼ oz. heavy cream
Blend with crushed ice and pour
into collins glass.

249. RED BIRD

1 oz. vodka
3 oz. tomato juice
Cold beer
Build in collins glass with cubed
ice. Fill with beer.

250. RED RUSSIAN

1 oz. vodka
½ oz. Cherry Heering
Build in rock glass with cubed
ice.

251. SALTY DOG

1¼ oz. vodka
Grapefruit juice
Build in salt-rimmed collins glass
with cubed ice. Fill with
grapefruit juice.

252. SCREWDRIVER

1¼ oz. vodka
Orange juice
Build in collins glass with cubed
ice. Fill with orange juice.

69

VODKA

253. SKIP AND GO NAKED

1¼ oz. vodka
1¼ oz. sweet-and-sour mix
Cold beer
Build in collins glass with cubed ice. Fill with beer.

254. SUNSTROKE

1 oz. vodka
2 oz. grapefruit juice
½ oz. triple sec
Blend with crushed ice. Pour into cocktail glass.

255. SWEET BANANA

1 oz. vodka
½ oz. créme de bananes
½ fresh banana
1 oz. sweet-and-sour mix
Blend with crushed ice. Pour into sour glass.

256. TEXAS BULLDOG

1¾ oz. vodka
¾ oz. Kahlúa
¾ oz. heavy cream
2 oz. cola
Build in collins glass filled 1/3 with cubed ice. Add cola. Watch it rise.

257. VODKA BLUE

1¼ oz. vodka
1½ oz. orange juice
1½ oz. pineapple juice
1 oz. sweet-and-sour mix
½ oz. blue curacao
Blend with crushed ice. Pour into collins glass. Garnish with red cherry.

258. VODKA COLLINS

1¼ oz. vodka
1½ oz. sweet-and-sour mix
7-Up
Build in collins glass with cubed
ice. Fill with 7-Up. Garnish with
red cherry.

259. VODKA GIBSON

1½ oz. vodka
½ oz. dry vermouth
Chill in mixing glass with cubed
ice. Stir and strain into martini
glass. Or build in rock glass with
cubed ice. Garnish with cocktail
onion.

260. VODKA GIMLET

1½ oz. vodka
½ oz. Rose's Lime Juice
Blend with crushed ice. Serve in
wine glass. Garnish with green
cherry.

261. VODKA HIGHBALL

1¼ oz. vodka
Soda, 7-Up, or tonic
Build in highball glass with cubed
ice. Fill with chosen mixer.
Garnish with squeeze of lime.

262. VODKA MARGARITA

1¼ oz. vodka
½ oz. triple sec
1½ oz. sweet-and-sour mix
¼ to ½ oz. fresh lime juice
Blend with crushed ice. Pour
into cocktail glass.

VODKA

263. VODKA MARTINI

1½ oz. vodka
½ oz. dry vermouth
Chill in mixing glass with cubed
ice. Stir and strain into martini
glass. Or build in rock glass with
cubed ice. Garnish with green
olive. Optional: lemon twist.

264. VODKA MELON

1¼ oz. vodka
½ cup diced, seeded watermelon
½ oz. pineapple juice
2 dashes of grenadine
Blend with crushed ice. Pour into
collins glass. Fill with cubed ice.

265. VODKA SLING

1¼ oz. vodka
1¾ oz. sweet-and-sour mix
½ oz. soda
¼ oz. cherry brandy (float)
¼ oz. grenadine (float)
Build in collins glass with
crushed ice. Add soda. Float
brandy and grenadine. Garnish
with red cherry.

266. VODKA SOUR

1¼ oz. vodka
1½ oz. sweet-and-sour mix
Blend with crushed ice. Pour
into sour glass. Garnish with
red cherry.

267. WHITE KNIGHT
1¾ oz. vodka
¾ oz. white créme de cacao
¾ oz. heavy cream
Build in rock glass with cubed
ice.

268. WHITE RUSSIAN
¾ oz. vodka
¾ oz. Kahlúa
½ oz. heavy cream
Build in rock glass with cubed
ice.

269. WHITE SPIDER
1¼ oz. vodka
½ oz. white créme de menthe
Build in rock glass with cubed
ice.

270. YELLOW-FELLOW
1 oz. vodka
½ oz. cointreau
2 oz. pineapple juice
Blend with crushed ice. Pour
into cocktail glass.

CREAM DRINKS

271. ALMOND-JOY
¾ oz. amaretto
¾ oz. white créme de cacao
1½ oz. heavy cream
Blend with crushed ice. Pour
into wine glass.

272. THE BAKER
¾ oz. rum
¾ oz. Tuaca
1½ oz. heavy cream
Blend with crushed ice. Pour
into wine glass.

273. BANANA BOAT
1 oz. créme de bananes
½ oz. orange juice
¼ oz. grenadine
1½ oz. heavy cream
Blend with crushed ice. Pour
into wine glass.

274. BANSHEE
¾ oz. créme de bananes
¾ oz. white créme de cacao
1½ oz. heavy cream
½ banana (optional)
Blend with crushed ice. Pour
into wine glass.

275. BIRD OF PARADISE
¾ oz. tequila
½ oz. white créme de cacao
¾ oz. amaretto
1¼ oz. heavy cream
Blend with crushed ice. Pour
into sour glass.

CREAM DRINKS

276. BLUE GOOSE
¾ oz. blackberry brandy
¾ oz. white créme de cacao
1½ oz. heavy cream
Blend with crushed ice. Pour
into wine glass.

277. BLUE MOON
1 oz. tequila
½ oz. Galliano
¼ oz. blue curaçao
1½ oz. heavy cream
Blend with crushed ice. Pour
into wine glass.

278. BLUE-TAIL FLY
½ oz. blue curaçao
¾ oz. white créme de cacao
1½ oz. heavy cream
Blend with crushed ice. Pour
into wine glass.

279. BRANDY ALEXANDER
¾ oz. brandy
¾ oz. dark créme de cacao
1½ oz. heavy cream
Blend with crushed ice. Pour
into wine glass. Garnish with
sprinkle of nutmeg.

280. BRANDY MELT
¾ oz. brandy
¾ oz. Kahlúa
1½ oz. heavy cream
1 egg white
Blend with crushed ice. Pour
into wine glass.

CREAM DRINKS

281. CHERRY FLIP
1¼ oz. cherry brandy
1 teaspoon sugar
1 egg
1½ oz. heavy cream
Blend with crushed ice. Pour
into wine glass.

282. CHERRY PIE
½ oz. Cherry Heering
½ oz. cherry brandy
¾ oz. white créme de cacao
1½ oz. heavy cream
Blend with crushed ice. Pour
into wine glass.

283. CHOCOLATE BANANA
½ oz. Vandermint
¾ oz. créme de bananes
½ oz. white créme de cacao
1½ oz. heavy cream
Blend with crushed ice. Pour
into sour glass.

284. COBRA
¾ oz. Galliano
¾ oz. amaretto
1½ oz. heavy cream
Blend with crushed ice. Pour
into wine glass.

285. COCONUT DREAM
¾ oz. white créme de cacao
¾ oz. créme de bananes
¾ oz. coconut milk
½ oz. heavy cream
Blend with crushed ice. Pour
into wine glass.

CREAM DRINKS

286. COFFEE, CREAM, AND SUGAR

¾ oz. coffee liqueur
¾ oz. white créme de cacao
1½ oz. heavy cream
Blend with crushed ice. Pour
into wine glass.

287. CREAM PUFF

1¼ oz. rum
1 teaspoon sugar
1½ oz. heavy cream
Soda
Blend with crushed ice. Pour
into wine glass. Fill with soda.

288. CRICKET

¾ oz. Vandermint
¾ oz. white créme de cacao
1½ oz. heavy cream
Blend with crushed ice. Pour
into wine glass.

289. 50-50 BAR

¾ oz. Galliano
¾ oz. triple sec
¾ oz. orange juice
1½ oz. heavy cream
Blend with crushed ice. Pour
into wine glass.

290. GOLDEN CADILLAC

¾ oz. Galliano
¾ oz. white créme de cacao
1½ oz. heavy cream
Blend with crushed ice. Pour
into wine glass.

CREAM DRINKS

291. GOLDEN DREAM
¾ oz. Galliano
¾ oz. white créme de cacao
½ oz. orange juice
1½ oz. heavy cream
Blend with crushed ice. Pour
into sour glass.

292. GRAND DE CACAO
½ oz. Grand Marnier
¾ oz. white créme de cacao
1½ oz. heavy cream
Blend with crushed ice. Pour
into wine glass.

293. GRASSHOPPER
¾ oz. green créme de menthe
¾ oz. white créme de cacao
1½ oz. heavy cream
Blend with crushed ice. Pour
into wine glass.

294. ITALIAN DREAM
¾ oz. Tuaca
¾ oz. Kahlúa
1½ oz. heavy cream
Blend with crushed ice. Pour
into wine glass. Garnish with
sprinkle of nutmeg.

295. ITALIAN STALLION
¾ oz. Galliano
¾ oz. créme de bananes
1½ oz. heavy cream
Blend with crushed ice. Pour
into wine glass.

CREAM DRINKS

296. LICORICE STICK
¾ oz. Pernod
¾ oz. anisette
Heavy cream
1 egg white
Blend with crushed ice. Pour into wine glass.

297. MERRY BERRY
¾ oz. blackberry brandy
¾ oz. triple sec
1½ oz. heavy cream
Blend with crushed ice. Pour into wine glass.

298. MEXICAN MILK SHAKE
½ oz. tequila
½ oz. vodka
¾ oz. Kahlua
1½ oz. heavy cream
Blend with crushed ice. Pour into wine glass.

299. PEACHY
¾ oz. peach brandy
¾ oz. white créme de cacao
1½ oz. heavy cream
Blend with crushed ice. Pour into wine glass.

300. PINK LADY
1 oz. gin
½ oz. sweet-and-sour mix
¼ oz. grenadine
1 oz. heavy cream
1 egg white
Blend with crushed ice. Pour into sour glass. Garnish with red cherry.

CREAM DRINKS

301. PINK SQUIRREL
¾ oz. créme de noyau
¾ oz. white créme de cacao
1½ oz. heavy cream
Blend with crushed ice. Pour
into wine glass.

302. POLAR BEAR
1 oz. vodka
½ oz. white créme de cacao
½ oz. heavy cream
Blend with crushed ice. Pour
into wine glass.

303. RED SNAPPER
¾ oz. rum
¾ oz. Galliano
¼ oz. grenadine
1½ oz. heavy cream
Blend with crushed ice. Pour
into wine glass.

304. RUM EXPERIENCE
½ oz. rum
½ oz. Galliano
¾ oz. white créme de cacao
1½ oz. heavy cream
Blend with crushed ice. Pour
into sour glass.

305. RUSSIAN BANANA
¾ oz. vodka
¾ oz. Kahlúa
1½ oz. heavy cream
1 banana
Blend with crushed ice. Pour
into sour glass.

CREAM DRINKS

306. SHORTY'S DESTROYER
1 oz. brandy
¾ oz. white créme de cacao
¾ oz. Kahlúa
1½ oz. heavy cream
Blend with crushed ice. Pour
into bucket glass.

307. SNOWBALL
¾ oz. gin
¾ oz. white créme de menthe
½ oz. anisette
1½ oz. heavy cream
1 egg white
Blend with crushed ice. Pour
into wine glass.

308. SNOW CONE
¾ oz. gin
¾ oz. green créme de menthe
1½ oz. heavy cream
Blend with crushed ice. Pour
into wine glass.

309. SUN DANCE
¼ oz. gin
½ oz. cointreau
¼ oz. anisette
¼ oz. white créme de menthe
1½ oz. heavy cream
Blend with crushed ice. Pour
into wine glass.

310. SWEET BRANDY ALEX
¾ oz. brandy
¾ oz. white crème de cacao
1 teaspoon sugar
1½ oz. heavy cream
Blend with crushed ice. Pour into
wine glass. Garnish with sprinkle
of nutmeg.

CREAM DRINKS

311. SWEET BRANDY BANANA ALEX

¾ oz. brandy
¾ oz. white créme de cacao
1 teaspoon sugar
1½ heavy cream
1 banana
Blend with crushed ice. Pour into bucket glass.

312. TOREADOR

¾ oz. tequila
¾ oz. white créme de cacao
1½ oz. heavy cream
Blend with crushed ice. Pour into wine glass.

313. TRADE WIND

½ oz. Grand Marnier
½ oz. Galliano
½ oz. apricot brandy
1½ oz. heavy cream
Blend with crushed ice. Pour into wine glass.

314. VELVET HAMMER

¾ oz. triple sec
¾ oz. white créme de cacao
1½ oz. heavy cream
Blend with crushed ice. Pour into wine glass.

UNIQUE SPECIALTIES

315. ALMOND STINGER

1 oz. amaretto
¼ oz. white créme de menthe
Build in rock glass with cubed ice.

316. AMERICANO

1 oz. Campari
1 oz. sweet vermouth
Soda
Build in collins glass with cubed ice. Fill with soda. Garnish with lemon twist.

317. ANGEL'S LIPS

¾ oz. Benedictine
¾ oz. heavy cream
Build in rock glass with cubed ice.

318. BANANA COFFEE

½ oz. créme de bananes
½ oz. dark créme de cacao
Coffee
Pour into coffee mug. Fill mug to ½ inch of rim with coffee. Garnish with whipped cream and red cherry.

319. BEAUTIFUL

¾ oz. cognac
¾ oz. amaretto
Build in rock glass with cubed ice.

320. CAFÉ ALMOND

½ oz. amaretto
¾ oz. Kahlúa
Coffee
Pour into coffee mug. Fill mug to within ½ inch of rim with coffee. Garnish with whipped cream.

UNIQUE SPECIALTIES

321. CAFÉ ROYALE

1¼ oz. bourbon
1 teaspoon sugar
Coffee
Pour into coffee mug. Fill mug
to ½ inch of rim with coffee.
Garnish with whipped cream.

322. CALYPSO COFFEE

¾ oz. rum
¾ oz. Kahlúa
Coffee
Pour into coffee mug. Fill mug
to ½ inch of rim with coffee.
Garnish with whipped cream
and red cherry.

323. CHERRY COFFEE

½ oz. Cherry Heering
½ oz. Kahlúa
Coffee
Pour into coffee mug. Fill mug
to ½ inch of rim with coffee.
Garnish with whipped cream
and red cherry.

324. CHOCOLATE COFFEE

¾ oz. Vandermint
¼ oz. dark créme de cacao
Coffee
Pour into coffee mug. Fill mug
to ½ inch of rim with coffee.
Garnish with whipped cream.

325. COCOA COFFEE

½ oz. dark créme de cacao
½ oz. white créme de cacao
Coffee
Pour into coffee mug. Fill mug
to ½ inch of rim with coffee.
Garnish with whipped cream.

UNIQUE SPECIALTIES

326. FAT CAT
½ oz. Galliano
½ oz. white créme de cacao
½ oz. cognac
1 scoop ice cream
Blend with crushed ice. Pour
into bucket glass.

327. GALLICE
½ oz. Grand Marnier
½ oz. Galliano
Build in rock glass with cubed
ice.

328. GORGEOUS
¾ oz. Grand Marnier
¾ oz. amaretto
Build in rock glass with cubed
ice.

329. GRAND COFFEE
½ oz. Grand Marnier
¾ oz. Kahlúa
Coffee
Pour into coffee mug. Fill mug
to ½ inch of rim with coffee.
Garnish with whipped cream.

330. GREEN LIZARD
1 oz. green chartreuse
¼ oz. 151-proof rum (float)
Serve straight up in pony glass.
Float rum. Optional: serve
flaming.

331. GUM DROP
¾ oz. Kahlúa
½ oz. anisette
Build in rock glass with cubed
ice.

UNIQUE SPECIALTIES

332. HARBOR LIGHT
¾ oz. Galliano
¼ oz. Metaxa (float)
Build in rock glass with cubed
ice. Float Metaxa. Serve flaming.

333. IRISH COFFEE
1¼ oz. Irish whiskey
1 teaspoon sugar
Coffee
Pour into coffee mug. Fill mug
to ½ inch of rim with coffee.
Garnish with whipped cream
and red cherry. Put dash of
green créme de menthe on
whipped cream.

334. ITALIAN STINGER
¾ oz. Tuaca
¼ oz. Galliano
Build in rock glass with cubed
ice.

335. KAHLÚA COFFEE
1½ oz. Kahlúa
Coffee
Pour into coffee mug. Fill mug
to ½ inch of rim with coffee.
Garnish with whipped cream.

336. KAHLÚA CREAM, OR MUDDY RIVER
1 oz. Kahlúa
½ oz. heavy cream
Build in rock glass with cubed ice.

UNIQUE SPECIALTIES

337. KEOKE COFFEE
¾ oz. brandy
¾ oz. Kahlúa
Coffee
Pour into coffee mug. Fill mug
to ½ inch of rim with coffee.
Garnish with whipped cream.

338. KING ALPHONSE
1 oz. dark créme de cacao
¼ oz. heavy cream
Serve straight up in pony glass.

339. KING OF HEARTS
½ oz. vodka
½ oz. Galliano
½ oz. Grand Marnier
1 scoop vanilla ice cream
Blend with crushed ice. Pour
into bucket glass.

340. LADYBUG
¾ oz. créme de bananes
¾ oz. triple sec
¾ oz. grenadine
Blend with crushed ice. Pour
into wine glass.

341. MEXICAN COFFEE
¾ oz. tequila
¾ oz. Kahlúa
Coffee
Pour into coffee mug. Fill mug
to ½ inch of rim with coffee.
Garnish with whipped cream.

UNIQUE SPECIALTIES

342. MOSS LANDING

¾ oz. Grand Marnier
¾ oz. créme de bananes
Coffee
Pour into coffee mug. Fill mug
to ½ inch of rim with coffee.
Garnish with whipped cream.

343. ORANGE JULIUS

1 oz. white créme de cacao
4 oz. orange juice
1 egg
2 teaspoons sugar
Blend with crushed ice. Pour into
collins glass.

344. ROOT BEER FLOAT

¾ oz. Galliano
1 oz. milk
Cola
Build in collins glass with cubed
ice. Fill with cola.

345. RUNNY NOSE

½ oz. Wild Turkey
½ oz. 151-proof rum
½ oz. green chartreuse
Build in rock glass with cubed
ice.

346. SCARLET O'HARA

1¼ oz. Southern Comfort
1½ oz. sweet-and-sour mix
¼ oz. grenadine
Blend with crushed ice. Pour
into sour glass. Garnish with
red cherry.

UNIQUE SPECIALTIES

347. SLOE COMFORTABLE SCREW

¾ oz. sloe gin
¾ oz. Southern Comfort
Orange juice
Build in collins glass with cubed
ice. Fill with orange juice.

348. SLOE SCREW

1¼ oz. sloe gin
Orange juice
Build in highball glass with cubed
ice. Fill with orange juice.

349. SPRITZER

3 oz. white wine
7-Up
Build in collins glass with cubed
ice. Fill with 7-Up. Garnish with
lemon twist.

350. TIGER'S TAIL

1 oz. anisette
Orange juice
Build in collins glass with cubed
ice.

351. TOOTSIE ROLL

¾ oz. dark créme de cacao
½ oz. orange juice
Build in rock glass with cubed
ice.

352. TOP HAT

¾ oz. cointreau
¾ oz. cherry brandy
Build in rock glass with cubed
ice.

UNIQUE SPECIALTIES

353. VENETIAN COFFEE
1¼ oz. brandy
1 teaspoon sugar
Coffee
Pour into coffee mug. Fill mug
to ½ inch from rim with coffee.
Garnish with whipped cream.

354. VERMOUTH CASSIS
1¼ oz. dry vermouth
¼ oz. créme de cassis
Soda
Build in collins glass with cubed
ice. Fill with soda.

355. WINE COOLER
3 oz. Burgundy
7-Up
Build in collins glass with cubed
ice. Fill with 7-Up.

356. YELLOW FEVER
¾ oz. yellow chartreuse
¾ oz. cognac
Build in rock glass with cubed
ice.

357. ZEBRA
¾ oz. Vandermint
¾ oz. heavy cream
Build in rock glass with cubed
ice.

INDEX

BAR TERMINOLOGY

BACK, CHASER
Mix or water served with the drink, but not in the drink.

BLEND
Mix in blender.

BUILD
Fill glass with ice and pour ingredients.

CHILLING GLASSES
Store glasses in refrigerator; or bury glasses in ice.

DASH
For all recipes in this book, a dash means approximately 2 drops.

DRY or VERY DRY
Little or no vermouth.

FLOAT
Ingredient lightly poured in circular motion on top of drink; used as a finishing touch.

GARNISH
There are two kinds: one, such as a twist, adds flavor and aroma; the other, such as an orange wedge, decorates the drink.

MIST
Liquor poured over crushed ice.

ON-THE-ROCKS
Over ice.

SHOT
In shot glass, usually 1 ounce.

SPLASH
Light touch of mix.

TALL
Tall glass, usually size of collins glass; allows for more mix.

TWIST
Piece of lemon rind rubbed on rim of glass and twisted to get rind flavor into drink.

UP
Drink made in mixing glass with cubed ice, stirred, and strained into martini or "up" glass.